LIFE WITH THE HOLY SPIRIT

DAWN YEOMANS

authorHOUSE®

AuthorHouse™ UK
1663 Liberty Drive
Bloomington, IN 47403 USA
www.authorhouse.co.uk
Phone: UK TFN: 0800 0148641 (Toll Free inside the UK)
*   UK Local: (02) 0369 56322 (+44 20 3695 6322 from outside the UK)*

Published by AuthorHouse 06/06/2022

ISBN: 978-1-6655-9908-5 (sc)
ISBN: 978-1-6655-9909-2 (e)

Print information available on the last page.

*Scripture quotations marked "NKJV" are taken from the
New King James Version. Copyright © 1982 by Thomas
Nelson, Inc. Used by permission. All rights reserved*

*Scripture quotations marked (NIV) are taken from the
Holy Bible, New International Version®, NIV®.
Copyright © 1973, 1978, 1984 by Biblica, Inc.™
Used by permission of Zondervan. All rights reserved worldwide.*

*Scripture quotations marked "ESV" are from the ESV Bible® (The Holy Bible,
English Standard Version®), copyright © 2001 by Crossway Bibles, a publishing
ministry of Good News Publishers. Used by permission. All rights reserved.*

This book is printed on acid-free paper.

INTRODUCTION

The purpose of this book is to help people find, then retain, the blessing of the Indwelling Holy Spirit. This is a blessing given by God. Personal investigation has shown that there is much information available, but little is accurate.

I have been blessed, and the Holy Spirit has led me to the Indwelling Father and Son, a further very rich blessing. This has brought me very close to God and Jesus. Each day my time is spent living and communicating with God and Jesus. This blessing is available to all of us. Hence it is God's will that I share some of my knowledge and experiences to help you all to draw close.

THE HOLY SPIRIT

The Holy Spirit is part of the Holy Trio. This consist of Almighty God (The Father), Jesus (The Son) and The Holy Spirit (The Holy Ghost). The Holy Spirit is a being.

Almighty God can bless Christians more than once on their spiritual journey. The first blessing is at the time of baptism/ christening etc., at the beginning of a Christian's spiritual life. At this point the Holy Spirit surrounds that person and guides them as they proceed on their journey. This is demonstrated by looking at,

John 1;32,33

Then John gave this testimony; 'I saw the Spirit come down from heaven as a dove and remain on him. And I myself did not know Him, but the one who sent me to baptise with water told me, "The Man on whom you see the Spirit come down and remain is the one who will baptise with the Holy Spirit". (NIV)

The Indwelling Holy Spirit is a blessing which can be given much later. Jesus made a reference to this blessing on his last evening before He died,

John 14:16,17

'And I will ask the Father, and he will give you another advocate to help you and be with you forever- the Spirit of Truth. The world cannot accept him, because it neither sees him or knows him. But you know him, for he lives with you and will be in you'. (NIV)

To avoid confusion, it is worth noting at this point that the disciples had already been baptised with the Holy Spirit As we can see at,

> *John 4;1*
>
> *-when Jesus learned that the Pharisees had heard that Jesus was making and baptising more disciples….(ESV)*

> *John 14;17*
>
> *But you know him for he lives with you….(NIV)*

After Jesus's death these same disciples were blessed and filled with the Holy Spirit as we can see from,

> *Acts 2;1,4*
>
> *When the day of Pentecost came, they were all together in one place…..*
>
> *……All of them were filled with the Holy Spirit… (NIV)*

This demonstrates that the Indwelling Holy Spirit is an additional blessing which is given post baptism.

In time it is possible for the Holy Spirit to dwell in a person's heart.

The Indwelling Holy Spirit is an experience and not just an intellectual theory. One can be very certain when the Holy Spirit is present. One can interact with the Holy Spirit. In time the Holy Spirit gradually reveals one's own spirit which can be felt. The spirit is quite sensitive and feels like part of the body.

HOW TO OBTAIN THE BLESSING OF THE INDWELLING HOLY SPIRIT

To my knowledge there are three methods available to obtain the blessing. These are,

(i)   Meditation and prayer
(ii) Prayer and general life changes
(iii) Laying of hands

For all methods, approaching Almighty God in prayer is the very first step.

> *Acts 1;14*
>
> *All these with one accord were devoting themselves to prayer... (ESV)*

(I) Meditation and Prayer

This is the method that I used. At the time I was totally unaware of the theology relating to the Indwelling Holy Spirit. I had read somewhere that it was possible to walk hand in hand with Almighty God, as in the Garden of Eden prior to the fall. Hence my personal motivation was to draw very close to Almighty God. My ignorance did initially hamper progress. This was soon resolved.

METHOD

Allow much time to approach and be with your Lord. In this society there is the inclination to cram much into our days, creating timeslots and so forth for all our activities. When approaching God, we need to be generous with our time and feel relaxed.

Meditation involves clearing our minds of everyday thoughts and activities. Initially this can be difficult to achieve. This does improve with practice. Before commencing with any meditation, we need to ask for protection. The following prayer could be used;-

O Lord, I pray that you would......
Surround me with the light of Jesus Christ,
Cover me with the blood of Jesus Christ, and
Seal me with the cross of Jesus Christ.
This I pray in the name of Jesus Christ.
Amen.
(Richard Foster, 2011)

Place yourself in a comfortable position such as sitting up on a bed. Clear your mind of any worldly thoughts and focus on a scriptural quotation relating to Jesus. This could include,

I am the light of the world
(Jesus is the light of the world)

I am the Good Shepherd
(Jesus is the Good Shepherd)

I am the gate
(Jesus is the gate)

Repeat such quotations many times until your mind is empty of the world. If the mind wanders, then return it to the quotation. When your mind is empty, think of being present in a scriptural scene involving Jesus. For example, sitting next to Jesus holding hands whilst his face shines as a bright light; or imagine that you are a sheep being carried by Jesus to a place of safety. Keep this going for some time.

I recall that I first felt the Holy Spirit's presence on my third attempt. With my eyes closed I saw a bright light, then felt the Holy Spirit breathing (regular breaths) on my face for some time. My initial reaction was not to let the Holy Spirit go. I would be taking time out to meditate and be with the Holy Spirit at every opportunity each day.

It would be worth mentioning at this point that everything can only be settled when put to prayer to Almighty God (i.e. nothing happens until you ask God). So, after the Holy Spirit has arrived, you would ask Almighty God in prayer for the Holy Spirit to remain with you.

Very soon the Holy Spirit is felt around the body and one's own spirit is gradually revealed. God's love is felt on one's spirit which is a personal and moving experience.

(II) PRAYER AND GENERAL LIFE CHANGES

Firstly, ask God in prayer for the blessing and ask to be shown what changes need to be made to your lives. At this point one would generally be maturing as a Christian. Daily this may include reading God's Word, praying regularly (perhaps upwards of three times a day), and generally attempting to live one's life by God's standards. This would include living by love,

> *1 Corinthians 13: 4-8*
>
> *Love is patient, love is kind. It does not envy, it does not boast, it is not proud. It does not dishonour others, it is not self-seeking, it is not easily angered, it keeps no record of wrongs. Love does not delight in evil but rejoices with the truth. It always protects, always trusts, always hopes, always perseveres. Love never fails...... (NIV)*

And living by the Spirit,

> *Galatians 5: 22-23*
>
> *But the fruit of the Spirit is love, joy, peace, patience, kindness, goodness, faithfulness, gentleness and self-control. Against these things there is no law. (ESV)*

Perfection is not necessary. The Holy Spirit will help you with this, at what ever point you are at, when he arrives. I would also point out that the Gospels show the disciples' many faults, up to the point of Pentecost, in no uncertain terms. However, reading the letters at the end of the New Testament shows very mature Christian men. The Holy Spirit will show you how to reach this level of maturity and beyond.

Now please consider the following,

> *Isaiah 55:8*
>
> *'For My thoughts are not your thoughts, neither are your ways My ways' declares the Lord. (NIV)*

1 Corinthians 1:20-21

Where is the one who is wise? Where is the Scribe? Where is the debater of this age? Has not God made foolish the wisdom of this world? For since, in the wisdom of God, the world did not know God through wisdom, it pleased God through the folly of what we preach to save those who believe. (ESV)

There is a huge difference between God's ways (Spiritual ways) and the world's ways. We are all familiar with the world's ways and know exactly how they work. God's ways (Spiritual ways) are very different and may seem illogical to our way of thinking. These ways have not been explained to us and just need to be accepted.

Finally, before proceeding, you will need to consider being prepared to give up absolutely everything for your 'pearl of great value' (Matthew 13:46). I intend to explain later the reason for this. As you live with the Holy Spirit, then later with the Spirit of God and Spirit of Jesus, every aspect of your life will be examined.

LIFESTYLE CHANGES

Please consider the following,

> *Matthew 6:24*
>
> *No one can serve two masters; for either he will hate the one and love the other, or else he will be devoted to one and despise the other. You cannot love God and money (ESV)*

> *1 John 2:15-17*
>
> *Do not love the world or the things in the world. If anyone loves the world the love of the Father is not in him. For all that is in the world- the desires of the flesh, the desires of the eyes, and the pride in possessions- is not from the Father but is from the world. And the world is passing away along with it's desires, but who ever does the will of God abides for ever. (ESV)*

One of the greatest obstacles to obtaining and retaining the blessing of the Holy Spirit is the world. I cannot stress this enough. In 2022 our lives are entrenched in the world:- our habits, our thoughts and preoccupations, our priorities, activities and aspirations. All these things drain us of love and distances us from Almighty God. Upon arrival the Holy Spirit will show what needs to be changed initially. In preparation I would suggest you do the following,

1. Turn off your televisions, mobile phones and laptops. Limit use to what is essential.
2. Avoid keeping up with the news.
3. Avoid discussing current affairs, health matters and other worldly topics.
4. Minimise retail purchases.
5. Empty your diary. Avoid rushing around to a busy schedule. You will need to spend much time with your Lord when He is with you.
6. Keep your home quiet and peaceful.
7. Simplify your diet. The Holy Spirit will show you things to avoid which all have spiritual implications. In preparation generally avoid sugar and processed food. Use fresh ingredients when possible.
8. Generally, simplify your life as much as possible. If this is something which needs attention, the following may help you,

Freedom of Simplicity. Richard Foster, 1981. Hodder & Staughton.

Hopefully, following the above will provide you with more time. This could be spent in prayer, reading God's Word and reading devotional material. Try to keep your thoughts away from the world. Keep Jesus and God frequently in your thoughts and, contemplate the scriptural material you are reading. Avoid any negative, unloving thoughts. It can be useful to repeatedly recite lines of scripture (e.g. from Psalms) to prevent the mind from wandering and to give constant prayer to God. Avoid any unloving words with those around you. When you do err, confess to Almighty God in prayer, as soon as possible. Also, consider that the Holy Spirit will make these things easy for you once He is in you.

(III) THE LAYING OF HANDS

Almighty God and Jesus can use someone with the Holy Spirit in situ, to give the blessing by the laying of hands. Almighty God and Jesus would need to be asked in prayer by both the person laying on hands and, the recipient. The laying of hands would need to be done privately in a quiet environment, in a prayerful manner. I would add that unless the changes in section (ii) have already been made the Holy Spirit would quickly leave.

THE INDWELLING HOLY
SPIRIT:- THE EARLY DAYS

There is a particular path to be followed from the time you feel the presence of the Holy Spirit, until you draw very close to Almighty God and Jesus. The purpose of the early days is for you to come to know the Holy Spirit and, for the Holy Spirit to eventually enter your heart. Everyone is different, but for me this took around 2.5 months. Incidentally, the Holy Spirit answers to the name Jesus. For the sake of clarity, I shall continue to refer to the Holy Spirit as Holy Spirit.

The early days are a time for establishing and strengthening your relationship with the Holy Spirit. This is a time when you will need to spend much time alone with the Holy Spirit EACH AND EVERY DAY. Initial changes are made to your habits and lifestyle. You will feel changes occurring within your body. You will want to pray more frequently and, you will be shown how to do this more effectively. Sadly, I am informed that the majority of Christians, who make contact with the Holy Spirit, never progress beyond this stage.

Once you feel the Holy Spirit's presence, He very quickly begins to work on your body to reveal your spirit. Your spirit is the means by which you can feel the love of God, Jesus and the Holy Spirit and, how they communicate with you. Your spirit is entwined throughout the whole of your earthly body. It can take several weeks for your spirit to be fully felt. An interesting scripture to consider is,

> *John 3:8*
>
> *The wind blows where it wishes, and you hear it's sound, but you do not know where it comes from or where it goes. So it is with everyone who is born of the Spirit. (ESV)*

You can feel the wind but cannot see it. You cannot see your spirit but you can certainly feel it. Your spirit feels very sensitive.

Once a part of your spirit has been revealed, the Holy Spirit pours love onto it. The purpose of this is for you to 'fall in love' with the Holy Spirit. The Holy Spirit cannot enter your heart until you love Him intensely. You will quickly come to appreciate that Almighty God is a God of love. In fact, I have been informed that Heaven is a place of love. Life there is spent with Almighty God, Jesus and the Holy Spirit loving Them All intensely.

The Holy Spirit quickly shows you how to pray. When commencing prayers, you will notice a noise in your ears. This is the sound of the Holy Spirit praying and, also Him talking to you in a loving way. The sound does become permanent. The Holy Spirit will indicate to you how to pray, especially the words and phrases to use and that which should be avoided. To put it simplistically, God and Jesus can respond to prayers when they are expressed correctly. When the same request is expressed incorrectly, it is harder for God and Jesus to intervene. The Holy Spirit will show you how to pray with your spirit and how to commune with God. Through communing with God, the Holy Spirit teaches you how to love God intensely. Later the Holy Spirit will show you how to love Jesus intensely.

The Holy Spirit will show you what initial changes you must make to your lives. This includes dietary changes, the pharmaceutical and toiletry products to avoid and, how exactly you need to be avoiding the world. These things I have outlined in the previous chapter. I do need to point out that if you are taking medication for a health condition, the Holy Spirit will show you exactly how to proceed. DO NOT suddenly stop taking your medication unless clearly told to do so.

I refer you to:

> *Matthew 4:1*
>
> *Then Jesus was led by the Spirit into the wilderness…..After fasting forty days and forty nights.……(NIV)*

After Jesus was baptised with the Holy Spirit he went into the wilderness to fast. Apparently, the main point was to fast from the world and it's distractions. I am informed that the main reasons why people loose contact with the Holy Spirit during these early days are their activities;- too much involvement and preoccupation with the world and not enough time spent alone with the Holy Spirit. From the time I felt the Holy Spirit around me, it was a good 2-2.5 months before I ventured into shops etc. In my past life I kept a very generous store cupboard. There was a good 2-3 months supply of food in the house including plenty to donate to the food bank. I hasten to add that the stocking up is not what God wants at all! But I hope that you are now beginning to see the picture. This time spent away from the world is required to draw much closer to God, Jesus and the Holy Spirit.

Most of what the Holy Spirit does for you is done by thought. Great levels of concentration are required. The worldly activities in which we involve ourselves are greatly distracting. It could be a likened to trying to pray a few inches away from someone using a pneumatic drill to dig up a road. This dries up the Holy Spirit's love and thus renders Him unable to work on you. Please do exactly what the Holy Spirit asks of you and stick to it.

It is possible for the Holy Spirit to become 'quiet' or to 'disappear'. This can be particularly distressing. This is another method of communication to show something is wrong. Either you have an unconfessed sin, a change needs to be made, or there is something else to which to reach out. As with all things, put this problem before God in prayer asking for forgiveness and guidance. Say how much you are missing the Holy Spirit. Return to the method of meditation if the absence becomes protracted.

Finally, these early days should be a time of great joy. I remember that I would want to be spending all my free time with the Holy Spirit and never be parted. Perhaps this is the level of commitment required for a close relationship and progression.

Throughout the early days, the stages to aim for are,

1. To ask Almighty God, Jesus and Jesus the Holy Spirit to abide in Jesus (the Holy Spirit)
2. A prayer of dedication giving everything to God, Jesus and the Holy Spirit.
3. A prayer asking Almighty God and Jesus to allow the Holy Spirit to enter your heart.

STEPS TO YOUR HEART

John 15:1-12

"I am the true vine and My Father is the vine dresser. Every branch in me that does not bear fruit he takes away, and every branch that bears fruit he prunes that it may bear more fruit. Already you are clean because of the word I have spoken to you. Abide in me and I in you. As the branch cannot bear fruit by itself, unless it abides in the vine, neither can you unless you abide in me. I am the vine, you are the branches. Whoever abides in me, and I in him, he it is that bears much fruit: for apart from me you can do nothing. If anyone does not abide in me, he is thrown away like a branch and withers; and the

branches are gathered and thrown into the fire and burned. If you abide in me, and my words abide in you, ask whatever you wish, and it will be done for you. By this My Father is glorified, that you bear much fruit and so prove to be my disciples.

"As the Father has loved me, so I have loved you. Abide in my love. If you keep my commandments, you will abide in my love, just as I have kept my Father's commandments and abide in his love. These things I have spoken to you, that my joy may be in you, and that your joy may be full. This is my commandment, that you love one another as I have loved you". (ESV)

1. ABIDE IN ME

John 15:4

Abide in me and I in you. (ESV)

A prayer to Almighty God is required around the time that your spirit has been fully revealed, the Holy Spirit has been pouring love onto your spirit and, when the Holy Spirit has been showing you how to pray. This would be to ask God and Jesus for permission for you to abide in Jesus (the Holy Spirit) and for Jesus (the Holy Spirit) to abide in you. At this time it would be loving if you told the Holy Spirit how you feel about Him.

The theology of this stage and beyond is explained succinctly in,

Abide in Christ. Andrew Murray. 1828-1917. Whitaker House.

2. CONSECRATION

Philippians 3:8-9

What is more, I consider everything a loss because of the surpassing worth of knowing Christ Jesus my Lord, for whose sake I have lost all things. I consider them garbage, that I may gain Christ and be found in Him….. (NIV)

Consecration:- Act of consecration, dedication.
                        Set apart as sacred, devote to.
(The Concise Oxford Dictionary, 1976)

This is the act of forsaking all and giving all;- in this case to Almighty God, Jesus and, the Holy Spirit. You would consider consecration when your relationship with the Holy Spirit is establishing. At this point you love the Holy Spirit deeply and do not want to be with out Him. By this time you have experienced an interval when the Holy Spirit has been "quiet" and realise how very painful this is. You have reached the conclusion that you are prepared to do anything and give up everything to feel the Holy Spirit's presence and, the love of God and Jesus.

The act of consecration would involve a prayer to God and Jesus. You would tell God and Jesus how you feel about the Holy Spirit. This would include telling God and Jesus that you want to give Them your life, yourself and body, your heart and love and, your mind. You would tell God and Jesus that you are prepared to give up anything. Clearly this is a solemn step and requires much thought.

I would add that giving God and Jesus your whole life means every moment and not just your free time or time slots.

At some point after your prayer of dedication, Almighty God seals the Holy Spirit to you. The seal is actually at the base of your head.

> *Ephesians 1:13*
>
> *.....when you believed, you were marked in him with a seal, the promised Holy Spirit, who is a deposit guaranteeing our inheritance until the redemption of those who are God's possession- to the praise of His glory. (NIV)*

The seal is the guarantee that the Holy Spirit will bring you to God and Jesus. However, the guarantee is only valid if you continue to do what the Holy Spirit advises.

3. ENTRY INTO YOUR HEART

This happens when you are full of love for the Holy Spirit and, after your prayer of dedication. This includes another prayer to Almighty God and Jesus asking Them to allow the Holy Spirit to enter your heart. When this occurs, you can actually feel the Holy Spirit enter the base of your heart (like something squashing into it). This is an experience and not just an academic theory. If you do not love the Holy Spirit enough this will not happen. Just persevere and continue with your loving relationship.

After entering you heart, the Holy Spirit circulates love throughout your spiritual blood vessels. This can be felt.

After the Holy Spirit has entered your heart, you will notice that He is no longer to be felt around your body pouring love onto it. This can be particularly distressing. The reason for this is that the Holy Spirit is now bringing you to Almighty God. You must now cultivate a deep love for Almighty God. The Holy Spirit will show you how to do this. Anything else would distract you at this point. You will renew a closer relationship with the Holy Spirit after God's Spirit and Jesus's Spirit have entered your heart.

In the mean time you can feel the Holy Spirit when you pray and commune with God. It is when you commune with God that you develop a close loving relationship with Him. It would assist progress if you were to read God's Word (eg Isaiah, Psalms) and to focus on God's qualities. Reading devotional publications would also be helpful.

DRAWING CLOSE TO GOD

Deuteronomy 6:5

Love the Lord your God with all your heart and with all your soul and with all your strength. (NIV)

John 14:16-17,23

And I will ask the Father, and he will give you another Helper, to be with you forever-the Spirit of truth.....

If anyone loves me, he will keep my word, and my Father will love him, and we will come to him and make our home with him. (ESV)

*A*fter having entered your heart, the work of the Holy Spirit is to bring you to Almighty God and then to Jesus. The Spirit of God cannot enter your heart until you love God intensely. This love would surpass that which you would feel for a husband or wife. Almighty God longs for a close and intimate relationship with each and every one of us. Something which is totally open and intensely loving. No doubt many of you will feel that this is a bit much or totally beyond you. Be reassured that the Holy Spirit can cultivate such a feeling within you and, make a close relationship with God possible.

When God's Spirit has finally entered your heart, the process is repeated for Jesus. It can take several months or years for God's Spirit to enter the heart. For me it took 7-8 months after I first felt the Holy Spirit's presence. For me, Jesus's Spirit followed 2-3 weeks later. Again, this is an experience and not just an intellectual theory.

This is a process that occurs over time. Life changes and circumstances can change. To make progress it is essential that you maintain daily contact with the Holy Spirit and can resolve any issues promptly. It is so easy to lose contact with the Holy Spirit. It is important to appreciate the reasons for this and to know how problems can be resolved.

DRAWING CLOSE TO GOD: EARLY MORNING PRAYER

Psalm 63:1

O God, You are my God
Early will I seek you........(NKJV)

Spending much time with God and Jesus early in the morning (or after awakening if you are a shift worker) is key to maintaining contact with the Holy Spirit and, developing your relationship with God. You would ask the Holy Spirit and God at what time you can pray early in the day. Stick to this unless circumstances change.

Matthew 6:6

But when you pray, go into your room, and when you have shut your door, pray to your Father who is in the secret place; and your Father who sees you in secret will reward you openly. (NKJV)

First of all you MUST BE ALONE. Go into a room where this is possible. Keep the same time each day. Allow enough time to spend unrushed, relaxed contact with God. The time does pass quickly.

Prior to praying it would be ideal to read a small section of scripture (eg about 5-10 minutes) and to have spoken some affectionate words to the Holy Spirit. Early in the morning your spirit is refreshed and responsive. The Holy Spirit also needs to rest regularly and is more refreshed at this time. Prior to prayer try to avoid any worldly activities or conversation. This would interfere with the quality of the time you spend with God and Jesus.

There are no specific instructions in the Bible, however I am informed that for prayer at home, for both men and women, it is essential to cover the head, torso and most of the limbs. The feet are to be kept uncovered (no shoes or socks). Standards of hygiene are to be observed.

During prayer you should speak through your mouth, not silently with your mind. God and Jesus need to hear you above any distracting thoughts or worldly noises. Speak slowly with gaps and wait for God to speak to you. Try to keep your mind free of any thoughts other than your communication with God and Jesus.

It may be helpful to consider,

> *Psalm 139: 5*
>
> *You have hedged me behind and before,*
> *And laid your hand upon me. (NKJV)*

Most of the time God is not far from us. In prayer God is usually sitting close to us. It took me so long to appreciate this fully. When you pray, in your mind speak to God with His face in front of you. Doing this helped me to progress.

For further reading,

Andrew Murray. The Inner Chamber. 1828-1917. Copyright 1981. Leona Frances Choy. CLC Publications.

DRAWING CLOSE TO GOD: COMMUNICATION

Acts 13:4

So, being sent by the Holy Spirit they went down to Seleucia...... (ESV)

Matthew 4:1

Then Jesus was led up by the Spirit into the wilderness.... (ESV)

The Holy Spirit will communicate with you in a specific way. This is to show, direct or warn. In my experience the most frequently used method is for the Holy Spirit to touch one's own spirit. The Holy Spirit will touch one part of your spirit to mean "yes" and a different part to mean "no". As you go about your day you will feel "yes" or "no" as you do or say certain things or, make certain choices. It is helpful to be still to receive any message accurately. As you draw closer to God, Jesus and the Holy Spirit, it is possible to ask God and Jesus questions and to receive a "yes" or "no" answer. You would need to ask an appropriate question with correct wording. This is how you can start to communicate directly with Almighty God and Jesus.

At this stage of your relationship, you will realise that the Holy Spirit can tire. In fact the Holy Spirit (and God's Spirit and Jesus's Spirit) need regular rests. As fleshly beings we take long sleeps (at night) and remain active for the whole day. The Holy Spirit has shorter bursts of activity and needs to rest (not sleep) more frequently. If possible, take 'power naps' or rests during the day. This helps the Holy Spirit to revive and continue to communicate with you. Your diet and other activities are also crucial for communication. You will very quickly want to rid yourself of any habit which hinders communication and sharing love with God.

When you communicate directly with Almighty God and Jesus, it would be done in prayer. You would choose a time of the day when the Holy Spirit is not tired. For example, not immediately after using a phone or computer. You will need to be loving and patient. As you draw closer to God it is possible to communicate more frequently. This very much depends on the love and affection you share with God and, the amount of time you spend daily with Him.

DREAMS

Once you have made your dedication the Holy Spirit has full access to your mind. Therefore, the Holy Spirit has control of your dreams. It is possible for the Holy Spirit to supply a dream as means of communication. It would be something about or additional to your daily experience or activities. For me such dreams have vivid colours and are usually symbolic and surreal. You will need to discus such dreams with Almighty God and Jesus. Do not rely upon your own interpretation.

DRAWING CLOSE TO GOD: GOD'S WILL

Ephesians 5:17

Therefore do not be foolish but understand what the will of the Lord is. (ESV)

Hebrews 10:36

....so that when you have done the will of God you may receive what is promised. (ESV)

*A*nother key step to drawing close to God is to seek God's will in all things. This would mean God's will in all our activities, from the trivial up to the major decisions. For this to be achieved effectively, it is helpful to be able to be able to communicate directly with God and Jesus. This is described in the previous chapter.

God wishes to share a very close relationship with every one of us. This involves being included with every aspect of our lives. After the Spirits of God and Jesus enter our hearts, they are sealed to us. God and Jesus need to be confident that we will not make any decision without consulting them first and, that we will do everything that They ask.

Now consider,

> 1 John 2:17
>
> …..*whoever does the will of God abides for ever. (ESV)*

In this world we are familiar with making our own choices. From the moment we awake we decide what to wear, eat and do during the day. In order to establish God's will, we would prayerfully discus our diary with God and Jesus, asking Them what They want us to do. We would include asking God and Jesus; what and when to eat: the routine of our day: and, our finances- what and how much to spend on various things including charitable contributions. Within these discussions you will find out exactly what God and Jesus want you to do and the changes which need to be made to your lives.

You would seek God's will concerning all earthly relationships. This would include those relating to family, friends, acquaintances and colleagues. If you were planning a wedding or starting a family, you would involve God and Jesus with these decisions.

When considering major decisions, you would put these before God and Jesus in prayer. For far reaching decisions you may want to confirm God's opinion on more than one occasion. You would refer to God and Jesus again with any changes. You would pray again after the decision has been made and delivered.

An important point is HOW you address God. Consider,

> *Matthew 18:3*
>
> *…..unless you turn and become like children, you will never enter the kingdom of heaven. Whoever humbles himself like this child is the greatest in the kingdom of heaven. (ESV)*

You would ask God's and Jesus's opinions and permissions as would a small child. You would avoid suggesting whenever possible.

DRAWING CLOSE TO
GOD: HUMILITY

1 Peter 5:6

Humble yourselves, therefore, under the mighty hand of God so that at the proper time He may exalt you........(ESV)

In order to draw close to Almighty God and Jesus, it is essential to be humble. By being humble we become nothing and in turn God and Jesus becomes our everything. In turn this becoming "our everything" is essential for our relationship with God and Jesus to blossom. The greatest example of humility is, of course, provided by Jesus.

Matthew 11:29

.......and learn from me, for I am gentle and lowly in heart.......(ESV)

Philippians 2:5-8

Have this in mind among yourselves, which is yours in Christ Jesus, who, though he was in the form of God, did not count equality with God a thing to be grasped, but made himself nothing, taking the form of a servant, being born in the likeness of men. And being found in human form, he humbled himself by becoming obedient to the point of death, even death on a cross. (ESV)

By reading God's Word we can see how Jesus achieved absolute humility and, what motivated Him. This is something we need to emulate in ourselves and our lives. We must be humble when before God and Jesus. In our lives and when interacting with others we need to be modest and humble. Our aspirations within this world should at least be modest.

Humility is a quality which takes many years to develop and can be a struggle to maintain. As with all things we can turn to God and Jesus in prayer when difficulties arise.

DRAWING CLOSE TO GOD: PRAYER THROUGHOUT THE DAY

1 Peter 3:12

For the eyes of the Lord are on the righteous,
And his ears are open to their prayer. (ESV)

*A*ny relationship with God and Jesus is one which involves prayer. Praying regularly throughout each and every day will draw you, and keep you, much closer to God and Jesus. Stopping regularly in the day to pray helps you to focus on spiritual priorities. Praying helps you not to become drawn into the world. By praying regularly, you will develop your love for God and Jesus and, you will never be far from them.

I personally pray upwards of five times daily. Unless circumstances change, I generally pray about the same time each day. My daily routine fits around my prayers and interaction with God and Jesus, not the reverse.

> *Philippians 4:6*
>
> *....but in everything by prayer and supplication with thanksgiving let your requests be made known to God. (ESV)*

I would also offer further prayers to God and Jesus. These would be when questions and issues arise during the day.

The prayer routine can involve different types of prayer and these could include Psalms and other Bible readings. For example, for me early morning prayer is one of personal requests and communing with God and Jesus. Later in the day I may wish to discuss other things. You may want to offer prayers of intercession. This could include bequests for others around you or, national or world issues.

James 5:16

The prayer of a righteous person has great power as it is working. (ESV)

Jude 20,21

….and praying in the Holy Spirit, keep yourselves in the love of God…..

All prayers offered through the Holy Spirit and Jesus are heard by Almighty God. To offer prayers of intercession with the Holy Spirit in situ is an effective way of asking blessings for others. To spend time on such an activity brings you closer to God and Jesus.

As your relationship with God and the Holy Spirit progresses, it is possible to commune with God at various times of the day. Communing with God requires much concentration from the Holy Spirit (and yourself). This is assisted by keeping contact with the world to a minimum and, maintaining your lifestyle habits as requested. Your relationship with God will deepen by communing regularly in the day.

Finally, I would mention that when God's Spirit and Jesus's spirit are within you, your prayer routine changes. To develop a routine of frequent daily prayers would assist with this transition.

DRAWING CLOSE TO GOD: THE MINISTRY

Matthew 28:19,20

Go therefore and make disciples of all nations, baptising them in the name of the Father and of the Son and of the Holy Spirit, teaching them to observe all that I have commanded you. (ESV)

John 12:26

.......If anyone serves me, the Father will honour him. (ESV)

Involvement with the ministry is another key activity which draws you closer to God and Jesus. However, God will tell you exactly what is required and when. After your consecration, the urge may be to submerge yourself with many religious or charitable activities. My understanding is that this is not what God wants. The early days are for establishing your relationship with the Holy Spirit and drawing closer to God and Jesus.

At the appropriate time the Holy Spirit will show you what to do. With me the ministry started slowly and gently. It is important that you do exactly what the Holy Spirit tells you. As with all things Almighty God has His reasons.

It is possible that you feel inexperienced or inadequate when considering the ministry. God will always put you in a situation in which He knows you are capable. At the appropriate time the Holy Spirit will fill you with so much love that nothing will seem insurmountable. I would point out that it is reaching into peoples' hearts that brings them closer to God. Clever theocratic arguments are more for the already converted.

DRAWING CLOSE TO GOD: WHEN GOD'S LOVE CANNOT BE FELT

There can be periods during which you cannot feel God's love. The duration and reason for this may depend on your stage of journey to God.

At the time you first feel the Holy Spirit's presence, or during the "early days", the Holy Spirit can suddenly become quiet. You are aware that you cannot feel the Holy Spirit around you. The main reasons are, unconfessed sin, the world or, not spending enough time with the Holy Spirit. This situation can become permanent if these issues remain unresolved.

After the Holy Spirit has entered your heart, there can be brief periods when you cannot feel God's love. This is upsetting. Again, the reasons for this can depend on your stage of progress. These I will now discus.

SIN

In this situation the first issue to consider is unconfessed sin. You would think carefully about your activities and what could be possibly wrong. You would pray to God and Jesus asking for forgiveness for anything which has caused offence. You would ask to be shown the problem. You would tell God how much you miss Him. When confessing sins, it would please God for you to discus each sin, and to be genuinely remorseful. You would ask to be shown how not to repeat the offence.

TIME WITH GOD

Not spending enough time with God and Jesus in prayer would be another issue to consider. It is easy to become absorbed with daily activities and to end up not praying as frequently. God understands when commitments and corresponding time constraints become a problem (though this would also be put before God and Jesus in prayer). However, being distracted with worldly activities is an issue.

THE WORLD

The world is one of the greatest reasons to be separated from God's love. Every day you need to be very aware of your activities and conversation, and to keep worldly contact to a minimum. For example, you would avoid discussing the news, local events and medical matters with other people. Doing so distances you from God's love, as these things dries up the love of the Holy Spirit. You are effectively choosing between God's love and doing these things. You would ask God and Jesus in prayer for help with this each day.

In 2022 retail activities such as the high street and online shopping features frequently in many people's daily tasks. These should be kept to a minimum.

When you do shop avoid large noisy supermarkets and shopping centres. Avoid browsing. Avoid the weekly shop. God prefers you to purchase a small number of items daily. As in the wilderness (Exodus 16), God will supply your needs each day. You would discus with God what and from where to buy. At a later stage, these short grocery outings provide opportunities for the ministry.

LIFESTYLE CHOICES

Prior to reaching God, we all have habits, commitments and lifestyle choices which distances us from God. God can use the quiet periods to alert you that a change is required. These would be discussed with God and Jesus in prayer.

God, via the Holy Spirit, asks you to omit certain items, foods, and lifestyle choices from your life. Should you deliberately ignore these requests, God will certainly be distant with you. God expects you to correct your habits and to make the changes permanent. If something is too difficult, it can be discussed with God in prayer.

NOISE

The Holy Spirit finds noise distracting. You would keep your home as quiet as possible. This would include keeping noise to a minimum when completing household chores such as food preparation. You would also avoid visiting busy noisy places, including those with overhead music, as much as possible.

TECHNOLOGY

Technology greatly distracts the Holy Spirit. You would avoid watching the television. You would keep usage of computers and phones to a minimum. You would ask God's permission before using these items.

SOCIALISING

Spending too much time with worldly other people can distance us from God. These people can be our family, friends, Christians and non-Christians. If you feel that this could be an issue, discus in prayer with God and Jesus.

LEISURE TIME

How we spend our leisure time can be an issue. I personally spend all my "free" time alone with God, Jesus and the Holy Spirit. Travel, going away on holiday or engaging with other worldly activities can distance us from God.

Finally, if we have become distracted or upset about something, God can use a silent period to quieten. A quiet period can also be used to indicate that there is something else to which to reach out. A quiet interval can also indicate lack of love when interacting with others.

HEALTH

1 Corinthians 12:4,9,11

Now there are varieties of gifts but the same Spirit…..to another gifts of healing by the same Spirit……..All are empowered by one and the same Spirit, who apportions to each one individually as he wills. (ESV)

Around the time of your consecration, the Holy Spirit takes full control of your body. God's will permitting, the Holy Spirit will protect you from all diseases and conditions. Spiritual laws begin. Worldly medical laws cease. Hence, it is so important to do exactly what the Holy Spirit tells you and to avoid the world as much as possible.

If you have a medical condition for which you are taking medication, the Holy Spirit will show you when and what to do. DO NOT stop taking your medication abruptly unless the Holy Spirit clearly indicates this. Any minor complaints would be put before God and Jesus in prayer. I usually pray, "I have problems with …….. May I leave this in your hands". Never refer to a worldly diagnosis. Only speak of the symptoms or problems.

Having been used to relying on medical science all our lives, the greatest obstacle is belief. If you doubt it will not work.

JUST BELIEVE.

I have remained totally well since my dedication.

THE FATHER AND THE SON

John 14:23

*Jesus answered him," If anyone loves me, he
will keep my word, and my Father will love
him, and we will come and make our home
with him." (ESV)*

The work of the indwelling Holy Spirit is to guide
you to God and Jesus. A mile stone has been passed
when God's Spirit and Jesus's Spirit enter your heart.

When you have reached the point that you love God
intensely and do not want to be apart from God, you
would approach God in prayer. You would express
your feelings and invite God into your heart. In
my experience, God's Spirit did not enter my heart

immediately, but later when I was distracted. God's Spirit could be felt squishing into the base of my heart. Almost immediately one is aware of more love radiating from the heart. Later, in prayer, God and the Holy Spirit tell you that God's Spirit has entered your heart.

God then guides you to Jesus. Communing changes and exercises are given to help you to quickly develop an intense love for Jesus. Almighty God does not want to be in your heart for very long without Jesus. Again, you would ask God in prayer for Jesus to enter your heart. Again, with me Jesus did not enter my heart immediately, but later when I was distracted with something else. The presence of Jesus's Spirit in your heart is confirmed later by God whilst in prayer.

Once God's Spirit and Jesus's Spirit are in your heart, God provides many exercises. The purpose of these is to help you to correct all your faults and weaknesses. Some of these exercises can be quite difficult.

Further changes to your habits and lifestyle are required. These are the final changes. As your love for God and Jesus increases, these changes become less of a problem.

The prayer routine changes. Within this routine you are required to take Holy Communion daily and, to ask Jesus to wash you each day. The daily experience of God's Spirit and Jesus's Spirit is profound. It is an immensely rich blessing.

Dear reader,

May Almighty God bless you and lead you to His eternal love.

REFERENCES

Holy Bible. English Standard Version. 2007. Crossway Bibles. HarperCollinsPublishers.

Holy Bible. New International Version. 2011. Zondervan

Holy Bible. New King James Version. 2015. Thomas Nelson, Inc

Richard Foster,2011: Sanctuary of the Soul. Hodder & Stoughton

The Concise Oxford Dictionary, 1976.Oxford University Press.

Printed in the United States
by Baker & Taylor Publisher Services